Bugs that Bite

Lice

by Pamela McDowell

MEDIA ENHANCED BOOKS

AV2 BY WEIGL™

ADDED VALUE • AUDIO VISUAL

www.av2books.com

AV² provides enriched content that supplements and complements this book. Weigl's AV² books strive to create inspired learning and engage young minds in a total learning experience.

Your AV² Media Enhanced books come alive with...

 Audio
Listen to sections of the book read aloud.

 Video
Watch informative video clips.

 Embedded Weblinks
Gain additional information for research.

 Try This!
Complete activities and hands-on experiments.

 Key Words
Study vocabulary, and complete a matching word activity.

 Quizzes
Test your knowledge.

 Slide Show
View images and captions, and prepare a presentation.

... and much, much more!

Go to www.av2books.com, and enter this book's unique code.

BOOK CODE

G795738

AV² by Weigl brings you media enhanced books that support active learning.

Published by AV² by Weigl
350 5th Avenue, 59th Floor
New York, NY 10118
Websites: www.av2books.com   www.weigl.com

Library of Congress Control Number: 2013953047
ISBN 978-1-4896-0770-6 (hardcover)
ISBN 978-1-4896-0771-3 (softcover)
ISBN 978-1-4896-0772-0 (single-user eBook)
ISBN 978-1-4896-0773-7 (multi-user eBook)

Printed in the United States of America in North Mankato, Minnesota
1 2 3 4 5 6 7 8 9 0   18 17 16 15 14

012014
WEP301113

Senior Editor Aaron Carr
Art Director Terry Paulhus

Photo Credits
Every reasonable effort has been made to trace ownership and to obtain permission to reprint copyright material. The publishers would be pleased to have any errors or omissions brought to their attention so that they may be corrected in subsequent printings.

Weigl acknowledges Getty Images as its primary image supplier for this title.

Bugs that Bite

Lice

Meet the Louse

A louse is tiny. This insect is only about 0.013 to 0.433 inches (0.33 to 11 millimeters) long. This is about the size of a sesame seed. The plural of louse is lice, and a group of lice is called a flock. Lice live on the bodies of people and animals. Most people think that lice are pests. This is because lice bite people and animals. Some lice can carry diseases that spread quickly.

Every year, 6 to 12 million people in the United States get head lice. Most of them are children.

Lice are found all over the world. They can even be found in Antarctica. Human lice are found wherever people live. Lice do not have wings to fly. They do not have strong legs to jump. They live their entire life on another animal. One African bird, the oxpecker, may eat lice. No other bugs or animals eat them. This means that lice are at the end of the food chain.

All About Lice

There are more than 3,000 species of lice. These species are divided into two main groups. The Anoplura are sucking lice. They live on mammals, including humans. Mallophaga lice chew or bite. Most Mallophaga live on birds. Only 15 percent of this group live on mammals.

Lice need only a small amount of blood to live. They need much less blood than a mosquito does. A louse, however, cannot live more than one or two days away from its host. The host is an animal that lice feed on. Lice can multiply very quickly. With proper treatment, an outbreak of lice can be controlled.

Archaeologists have found signs of lice on mummies in Egypt.

Types of Lice

Anoplura

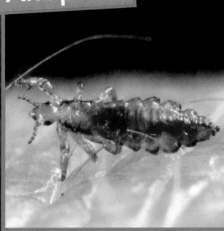

- Made up of about 500 species
- Is a sucking louse
- Have mouthparts that can pierce skin
- Include three kinds of human lice, including head lice
- Are known to spread deadly diseases among humans

Mallophaga

- Feeds on blood found in feathers and skin
- Made up of more than 2,600 species
- Have biting mouthparts that are called **mandibles**
- Cannot survive on humans
- Have well-developed claws for clinging to host
- Have a flattened, wingless body, usually eyeless

Lice
Habitats

Lice depend on animals and birds for food and warmth. Each different species of lice lives on one kind of animal. For example, lice that live on hummingbirds cannot live on cows. Lice that live on chickens cannot live on humans. The host animal becomes the louse's habitat.

The elephant louse can only survive on elephants. It has tough skin to protect it from the heat and Sun. Its mouthparts are sharp enough to pierce the elephant's thick skin.

Each kind of lice has **adapted** to its habitat. A louse may have claws that help it hold onto a hair. The louse may be white, yellow, brown, black, or even red. This depends on the color of the host's skin, fur, or feathers. It is possible for several kinds of lice to live on one host.

Female lice are larger than males. There are usually many more female lice than male lice on a host. If the host animal is not able to groom itself, lice will multiply quickly. A duck with an injured bill is unable to remove lice and **nits**. The duck could soon be covered with thousands of lice.

A bird can have four or five kinds of lice living on different parts of its body.

Typical Louse
Features

THORAX

The thorax is the part of the body between the head and the abdomen. In some lice, the thorax has three distinct segments. In the Anoplura louse, it is a single part protected by a body plate on top.

ABDOMEN

The abdomen is the largest part of the louse. It is made up of 8 to 10 segments. There are small openings called **spiracles** on the bottom of the abdomen. The louse takes in air through the spiracles.

LEGS

Six short legs are attached to the thorax. They often have claws that can grab and hold onto hairs.

HEAD

Lice have two short antennae on their heads. The antennae help the louse detect gases released by the host's skin. This way the louse finds its correct host species.

MOUTH

The mouth has unique parts for biting or sucking. A chewing louse gnaws the host's skin. A sucking louse has three **stylets** that pierce the skin of the host and inject saliva. Blood is sucked through the stylets. The stylets are stored inside the head when they are not being used.

EYES

The eyes of louse are sensitive to light. This is one reason lice prefer to live on the skin, under feathers and fur. The eyes may not be developed because the louse does not need to see to find a host. Some species of lice do not have eyes.

Lice
Life Cycle

Most lice spend their entire life cycle on the animal host. After a female louse mates, she lays her eggs on the skin, hair, or feathers of the host. She continues to feed on the host's blood and lay eggs. She may lay between 50 and 100 eggs in her lifetime. Head lice can lay up to four eggs a day. Only human body lice will leave the host to lay eggs.

There are three stages in a louse's life cycle: egg, **nymph**, and adult. Adults live between 30 and 40 days, depending on the species. They cannot live without a host. They cannot live in bedding or clothing without a fresh supply of blood.

The adult female louse feeds on the host before laying her eggs.

Stage 1
Eggs

A female louse may lay her eggs singly or in clumps. The eggs are called nits. They are about 0.06 inches (1.5 mm) long. She cements the nits to a feather or hair. The nits will hatch in 6 to 14 days.

Nymphs

Newly hatched lice are called nymphs. Some nymphs use a sharp growth on their heads to hatch from the egg. Other nymphs suck air into the nit until it bursts open. When the nymph hatches, it is colorless and smaller than an adult. A nymph must feed within 24 hours of leaving the egg or it will die. During **metamorphosis**, the nymph will molt, or shed its skin, three times. Each time, the nymph becomes larger and looks more like an adult. This stage takes between 8 and 16 days.

Stage 3
Adults

After the third molt, the nymph has developed into an adult. The louse is attracted to warm parts of the host's body. The louse will use its claws to attach itself to the host's hair or feathers, close to the skin. It feeds on the host, and a female lays her eggs there. The life cycle begins again.

13

How do Lice Bite?

A louse moves around on its host. It will bite many times in its search for fresh blood. Lice drink blood in two different ways, depending on the species. A sucking louse will pierce the host's skin with its stylets. Some of the louse's saliva will flow into the wound. This special saliva keeps the blood thin and easy to suck.

Blood sucked from the host animal is stored in the louse's abdomen.

Chewing lice use mandibles to bite through the host's skin. The mandibles may move up and down or from side to side. Like sucking lice, chewing lice use saliva to prevent the wound from healing quickly. Chewing lice also feed on the blood in the shafts of feathers and on loose bits of skin.

Parts of a Louse

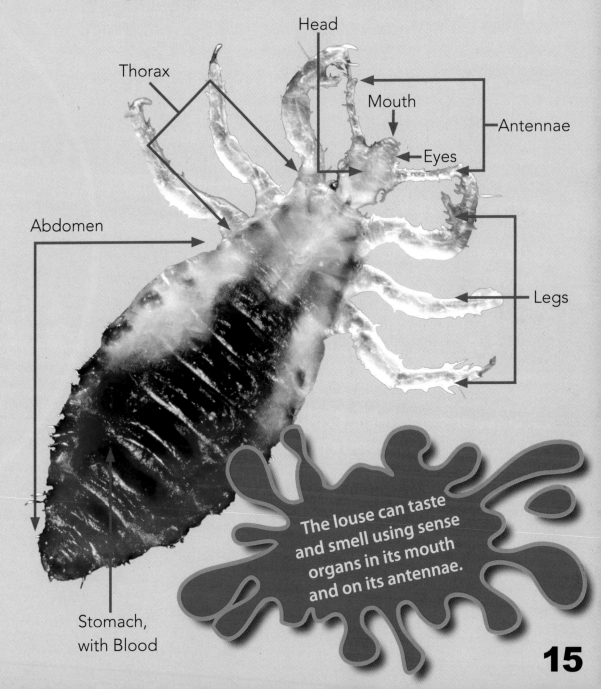

Head

Thorax

Mouth

Antennae

Eyes

Abdomen

Legs

Stomach, with Blood

The louse can taste and smell using sense organs in its mouth and on its antennae.

Lice and Disease

Typhus is one of the worst diseases in human history. It has been affecting humans for centuries. In 1909, a French doctor proved that the disease was carried by lice. He proved that human body lice spread deadly **bacteria** that covered clothing and bedding. This bacteria, called rickettsia, caused headaches, chills, fever, and death. About a week after a person was infected with the disease, a rash covered the person's body. Next came a very high fever. After another week, a person who had been weak or unhealthy before catching the disease usually died.

At the end of World War I, an outbreak of **epidemic** typhus resulted in several million deaths. During World War II, there were again deadly outbreaks of this disease. Crowded, dirty living conditions and the lack of healthy food helped spread the disease. Millions of people in Europe died. Today, typhus is treated with drugs, **vaccinations**, and **insecticides**. Epidemic typhus is not found in **developed countries**.

One type of fever, called a relapsing fever, is also spread by human body lice. This fever is called relapsing because it returns many times after a person feels better.

Relapsing fever killed **5 million** people in Europe between **1919** and **1923**.

Epidemic **typhus** is still found in **Africa**, **Asia**, and **Central** and **South America**.

Without treatment, up to **60%** of people with epidemic typhus may die.

Dr. Charles-Jules-Henri Nicolle received the **Nobel Prize** in **1928** for discovering the cause of epidemic typhus.

Trench fever is spread by lice, but it rarely causes death.

People may shave their heads to get rid of lice.

Treating Bites

In North America, head lice cause the most problems. The bites from these lice may not be noticed at first. Very soon, though, the bites form tiny red spots on the person's skin. This is a reaction to the saliva that lice inject into the bites. These spots are very itchy. Head lice do not carry diseases. The bites, however, can become infected if they are scratched too much.

Lice and nits cling firmly to hair. Some may be removed using a fine-toothed comb. It is best to see a doctor or other qualified health practitioner to treat lice. Treatments usually include shampoos or lotions containing an insecticide that will kill the lice and nits.

Some people try to kill lice by covering their hair with mayonnaise. This **home remedy** has not been proven to work.

Head lice are very contagious. This means it is easy to catch them from someone else. Lice cannot jump or fly. They spread by direct contact, such as head-to-head contact. Sharing combs, hats, helmets, or pillowcases can also spread lice.

Birds control lice by **preening**. A bird's bill acts like a fine-toothed comb to remove lice and nits. Dust baths help some animals control lice. Pets and livestock, such as cattle and horses, are sprayed with an insecticide to kill lice.

Spraying or shampooing hair with products that contain insecticides is the most effective way to get rid of head lice.

About 80 percent of schools in North America have an outbreak of lice every year.

Myths and Legends

Myths and legends about lice are told around the world. An **Inuit** legend tells the story of two sisters who were outside, enjoying a calm winter day. They began to pick lice from each other's hair and drop them in the snow. The weather turned stormy. Thick snow flew around the sisters. They became lost in the snowstorm. Ever since, Inuit children are warned never to remove lice outdoors because it will cause a storm.

In South China, there is a legend about Pan Gu, the ancestor of mankind. When he died, it is said that his breath became the wind and clouds. One eye became the Moon. The other eye became the Sun. His body and limbs became mountains, and his tears flowed to make rivers. The fleas and lice on his body became the ancestors of humans.

Charting a Lice Food Chain

Lice are not a source of food. They are at the end of the food chain. In this activity, create a chart that shows the louse food chain.

Materials you will need:  Two sheets of paper   Pencil

Activity

1 Fold one sheet of paper in half so the top and bottom edges are together. Then, fold it one more time the same way. When you open the paper, you should have four horizontal sections to form your chart.

2 Put the sucking louse in the top section. In the section below that, choose a carnivore that may be a host for the louse.

3 Research the kind of herbivores this carnivore might eat. Write these in the third section. Research what producers the herbivore might eat. Record this in the bottom section of your chart.

4 On your second sheet of paper, illustrate this food chain. Use arrows to show the connection between producers, herbivores, carnivores, and lice.

5 Create a food chain for the chewing louse. How do the food chains for a sucking and chewing louse differ?

Know Your Stuff

Use the book to answer these questions about lice.

1 How big is a louse?

2 How many species of lice are there?

3 What are the two groups of lice?

4 What is a host?

5 Which is larger, the female louse or the male louse?

6 About how many people in the United States get head lice every year?

7 How does a louse hang onto its host?

8 What are the stages of a louse's life cycle?

9 How is epidemic typhus spread?

10 How can a person get rid of head lice?

Answers:
1. About the size of a sesame seed 2. More than 3,000 3. Sucking and chewing 4. The animal on which a louse lives and feeds 5. Female 6. 6 to 12 million 7. Its claws grab hairs or feathers 8. Egg (nit), nymph, and adult 9. Through lice that carry bacteria 10. Use shampoo with insecticide

Key Words

adapted: changed to fit into a new habitat

archaeologists: scientists who study old objects, bones, and buildings to learn about the past and understand how people lived

bacteria: tiny living things made of a single cell

developed countries: countries where most people have relatively high standards of living

epidemic: a quick spreading of a disease to a large number of people at the same time

home remedy: a cure that uses items found around the house rather than medicines

insecticides: harmful chemicals used to kill insects

Inuit: a native person of northern Canada and Alaska

mandibles: the paired jaws of an insect that are used for biting and chewing

metamorphosis: a series of changes in form as an insect becomes an adult

nits: the eggs of a louse

nymph: a young insect that has not yet grown into an adult

preening: when a bird cleans its feathers with its beak

spiracles: the holes an insect uses to take in air

stylets: needle-shaped mouthparts used for cutting and sucking juices

vaccinations: drugs that will protect people from diseases

Index

Log on to www.av2books.com

AV² by Weigl brings you media enhanced books that support active learning. Go to www.av2books.com, and enter the special code found on page 2 of this book. You will gain access to enriched and enhanced content that supplements and complements this book. Content includes video, audio, weblinks, quizzes, a slide show, and activities.

AV² Online Navigation

Book Pages
AV² pages directly correspond to pages in the book.

Audio
Listen to sections of the book read aloud.

Video
Watch informative video clips.

Key Words
Study vocabulary, and complete a matching word activity.

Embedded Weblinks
Gain additional information for research.

Quizzes
Test your knowledge.

Slide Show
View images and captions, and prepare a presentation.

Try This!
Complete activities and hands-on experiments.

AV² was built to bridge the gap between print and digital. We encourage you to tell us what you like and what you want to see in the future.

Sign up to be an AV² Ambassador at www.av2books.com/ambassador.